Theory for Young Musicians

Theory Lessons • Ear Training • Worksheets

Table of Contents

Nathaniel Gunod
Susan Mazer

This book was acquired, edited and produced by Workshop Arts, Inc., the publishing arm of the National Guitar Workshop.
Nathaniel Gunod, acquisitions, editor
Michael Rodman, editor
Gary Tomassetti, music typesetter
Timothy Phelps, interior design
Barbara Smolover, interior illustrations
CD recorded at Bar None Studios, Northford, CT

Photos:
Violin courtesy of Scherl & Roth/United Musical Instruments U.S.A., Inc.
Guitar courtesy of Martin Guitar Company
Boy, lower left: © 2001 RubberBall Productions

Introduction

By now, you have either completed the Notespeller and Book 1 of *Theory for Young Musicians*, or you know beginning theory pretty well. If you know about whole steps and half steps, the major scale, key signatures and eighth notes and eighth rests, you are ready to begin Book 2.

This book works just like Book 1 did. There are lessons, worksheets and ear-training exercises with examples on the CD. You will learn about the circle of 5ths, the order of sharps and flats in key signatures, triads, dotted rhythms, § time, dynamics and more.

The more you know about music, the more fun you will have playing your instrument. We hope you will be playing and learning about music for many years. Keep your ears wide open and listen to as many different kinds of music as you can. Most importantly, keep having fun!

About the Authors

Nat Gunod is the chief editor for Workshop Arts, Inc., the publishing arm of the National Guitar Workshop. He is the author of *Classical Guitar for Beginners, Renaissance Duets: Play Along Library, Progressive Classical Solos* and *Theory for Guitar Made Easy*. Nat is an Associate Director of the National Guitar Workshop and directs the NGW Classical Guitar Seminar. He has performed all over the United States and taught students from all over the world at the Workshop and at various colleges, including the Peabody Conservatory of the Johns Hopkins University.

Philadelphia-born **Susan Mazer** lives and works in Connecticut. Susan, who received her Bachelor of Music degree from the Hartt School of Music, is on the faculty of the Hartford Conservatory, where she teaches theory and ear training. Since 1989 Susan has taught fingerstyle guitar at the National Guitar Summer Workshop. She has performed with an acoustic duo for the last fifteen years, and is the author of several books, including *Guitar for the Absolute Beginner* and *Learn to Sing and Play Guitar.*

Track 1

The CD that accompanies this book can make learning with the book easier and more enjoyable. All the ear-training exercises in the book are on the CD, and all include include demonstrations or practice examples. Feel free to pause the CD as you work on the exercises, or to listen to tracks more than once. The symbol at left, which appears next to each exercise, shows you which track to listen to. Track 1 will help you tune your electronic keyboard or guitar to this CD.

Before We Begin:
Keyboard & Fretboard Diagrams

Throughout this book, you'll see keyboard and fretboard diagrams that will make learning easier. The keyboard diagrams look just like a section of the piano keyboard. The fretboard diagrams show you the frets and strings of the guitar. Dots on the fretboard diagram show you which fret and string to use.

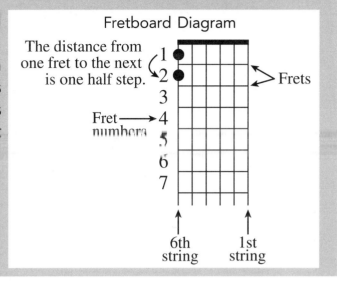

Fretboard Diagram

The distance from one fret to the next is one half step.

Fret numbers

Frets

6th string

1st string

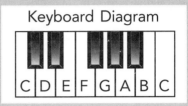

Keyboard Diagram

C D E F G A B C

The Circle of 5ths

It's easy to count to five, and it's easy to imagine a circle. This means that understanding one of the most important ideas in music theory—the circle of 5ths—is easy!

Begin on the note C and count up five notes through the C Major scale. This will put you on G. The distance from C to G is called a 5th.

Now, begin on G and count up five notes through the G Major scale. This will put you on D. The distance from G to D is also a 5th.

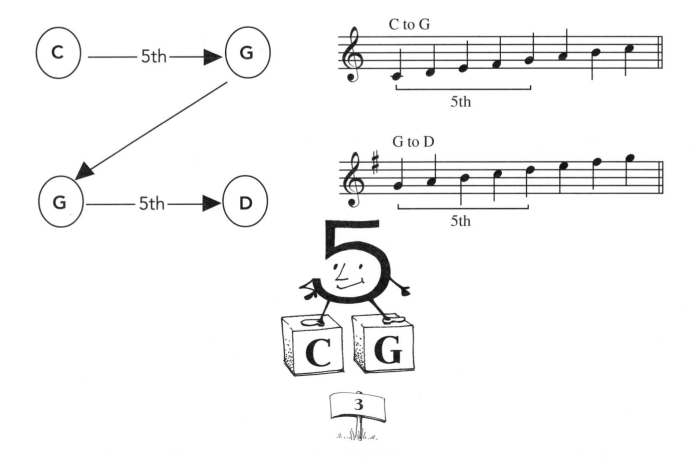

C —— 5th ——▶ G

G —— 5th ——▶ D

C to G

5th

G to D

5th

Each of the letters in the circle of 5ths is also the name of a key. For now, try to learn the order of the notes in the circle of 5ths.

You already know that some notes, like F♯ and G♭, or C♯ and D♭, are enharmonic—they sound exactly the same but have different names. Some keys on the circle of 5ths work the same way. The keys of F♯ and G♭ are enharmonic, and so are C♯ and D♭. The notes that make up enharmonic keys sound the same but have different names.

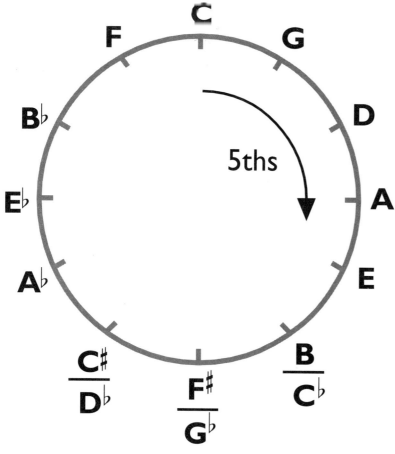

WORKSHEET

- Write out the major scale that begins on each note.

- Write the name of the major scale to the right of each example.

- Name the distance from the tonic of one scale up to the tonic of the next.

Example:

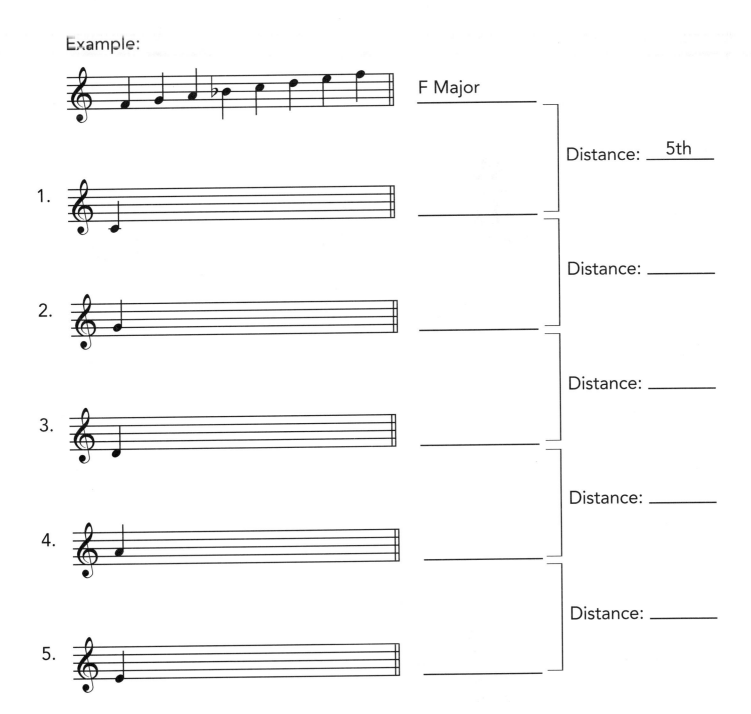

F Major

Distance: ___5th___

1.

Distance: _____

2.

Distance: _____

3.

Distance: _____

4.

Distance: _____

5.

Distance: _____

EAR TRAINING

A
TRACK
2

- Listen to the following major scales.
- Sing along using the syllables you learned in Book 1 (Do Re Mi Fa Sol La Ti Do).

1.

Do Re Mi Fa Sol La Ti Do

2.

Do Re Mi Fa Sol La Ti Do

3.

Do Re Mi Fa Sol La Ti Do

B
TRACK
3

- Listen to each pair of notes.
- If the distance between them is a 5th, circle "5th."
- If the distance is smaller than a 5th, circle "Smaller."
- If the distance is larger than a 5th, circle "Larger."

Example: (5th) Smaller   Larger

1.   5th   Smaller   Larger

2.   5th   Smaller   Larger

3.   5th   Smaller   Larger

4.   5th   Smaller   Larger

5.   5th   Smaller   Larger

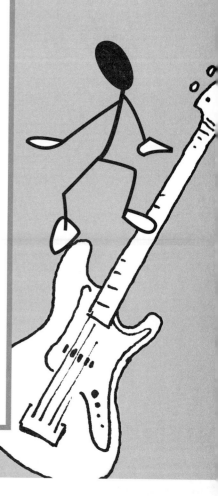

The Order of the Keys

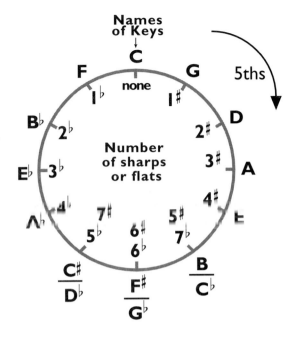

Knowing the circle of 5ths can help make learning key signatures easy. Here's another picture of the circle of 5ths, this time showing how many sharps or flats are in each key:

When sharps appear in a key signature, they always appear in this order:

F C G D A E B

This means that if a key signature has two sharps, they will always be F♯ and C♯; if it has three sharps, they will always be F♯, C♯ and G♯; and so on. You can use this phrase to help you remember the order of sharps in the key signature:

Fat **C**ows **G**o **D**own **A**nd **E**at **B**reakfast

Here's a trick for reading major key signatures with sharps:

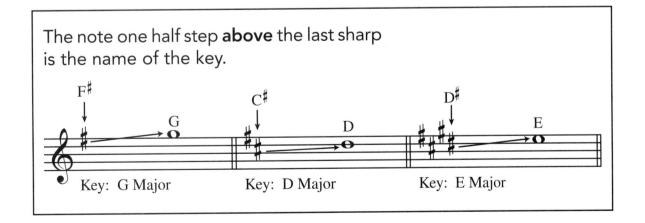

The note one half step **above** the last sharp is the name of the key.

F♯ → G — Key: G Major

C♯ → D — Key: D Major

D♯ → E — Key: E Major

When flats appear in a key signature, they always appear in this order:

This means that if a key signature has two flats, they will always be B♭ and E♭; if it has three flats, they will always be B♭, E♭ and A♭; and so on. You can use this phrase to help you remember the order of flats in the key signature:

Be **E**ver **A**lert **D**uring **G**uitar **C**lass, **F**riend

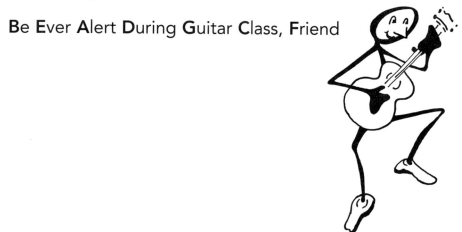

Here's a trick for reading major key signatures with flats:

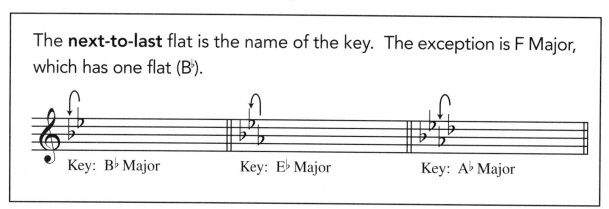

The **next-to-last** flat is the name of the key. The exception is F Major, which has one flat (B♭).

Key: B♭ Major   Key: E♭ Major   Key: A♭ Major

WORKSHEET

- Write out the correct key signature in each staff.

- To find key signatures with sharps, think of the order of the sharps, and find the name of the sharp that's one half step **below** the name of the key you want. All the sharps up to and including this one will give you the key signature. Remember that the note one half step **above** the last sharp gives you the name of the key signature.

- To find key signatures with flats, think of the order of the flats, and go one flat **past** the flat with name of the key you want. All the flats up to and including this one will give you the key signature. Remember that the second-to-last flat gives you the name of the key signature.

- Watch out for clef changes!

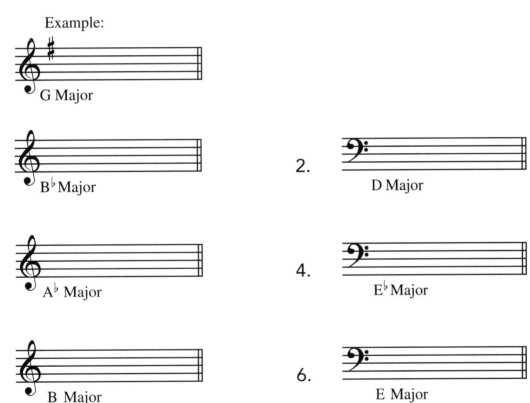

EAR TRAINING

- Sing the original melody on "La."
- In 1, 2 and 3, sing the same melody in the given keys.
- Write the name of the key below each example.

Original melody:

G Major

1.

Key: _____

2.

Key: _____

3.

Key: _____

- Listen to each example.
- Circle the letter of the melody that matches each example you hear.
- Circle all the 5ths you find in the music.

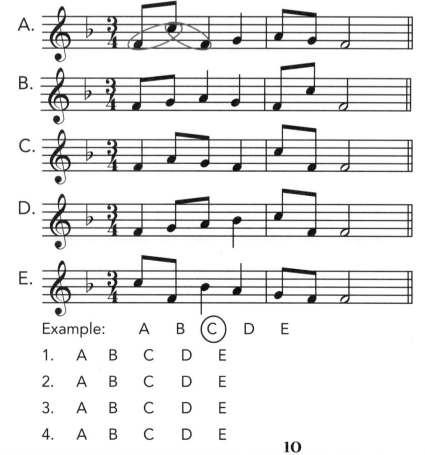

Example: A   B   Ⓒ   D   E
1.   A   B   C   D   E
2.   A   B   C   D   E
3.   A   B   C   D   E
4.   A   B   C   D   E

Intervals— Major and Perfect

An **interval** is the difference in pitch between two notes. You already know one way of measuring the distance between two notes: counting the half steps. A whole step, for example, is made up of two half steps.

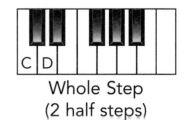

Whole Step
(2 half steps)

On pages 3 and 4 of this book, you learned about the circle of 5ths. The distance from one note to the next in the circle—C to G, G to D, D to A, and so on—is always the same. This interval, made of seven half steps, is called a **perfect 5th**.

Perfect 5th
(7 half steps)

There are two ways to play an interval. If you play the notes one at at a time, it is called a **melodic interval**. If you play both notes of an interval at the same time, it is called a **harmonic interval**.

Perfect 5th   Perfect 5th
Melodic   Harmonic

Let's look at the major scale—we'll use C Major—and the intervals in it, measured from the root. Each of these intervals is either a **major** or a **perfect** interval. By numbering the notes in the scale from 1 to 8, it's easy to learn the intervals. Just count up to each note from the root to learn the number name of the interval! Notice that the interval between a note and itself is called a **unison**. The interval between a note and the next highest note with the same name is an **octave**.

Intervals built on the notes of the C Major scale

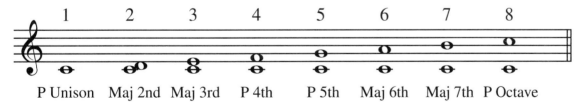

P Unison   Maj 2nd   Maj 3rd   P 4th   P 5th   Maj 6th   Maj 7th   P Octave

Maj = Major
P = Perfect

Since the number of half steps in an interval always remains constant, memorizing the number of half steps is another way to identify intervals.

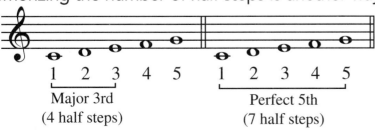

Major 3rd   Perfect 5th
(4 half steps)   (7 half steps)

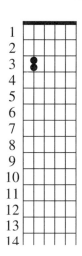

- The distance from C to itself is 0 half steps
- C is the first note in the scale.
- This interval is a **perfect unison.**

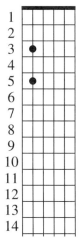

- The distance from C to D is two half steps.
- D is the second note in the scale.
- This interval is a **major 2nd**.

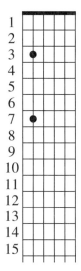

- The distance from C to E is is four half steps.
- E is the third note in the scale.
- This interval is a **major 3rd**.

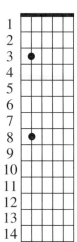

- The distance from C to F is five half steps.
- F is the fourth note in the scale.
- This interval is a **perfect 4th**.

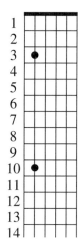
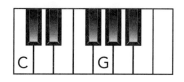

- The distance from C to G is seven half steps.
- G is the fifth note in the scale.
- This interval is a **perfect 5th**.

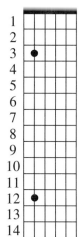

- The distance from C to A is nine half steps.
- A is the sixth note in the scale.
- This interval is a **major 6th**.

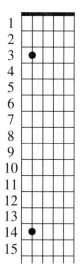
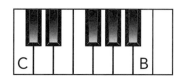

- The distance from C to B is eleven half steps.
- B is the seventh note of the scale.
- This interval is a **major 7th**.

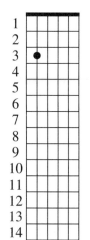

- The distance from C to C is twelve half steps.
- C is the eighth note of the scale.
- This interval is a **perfect octave** (not a perfect 8th!).

WORKSHEET

A
- Write the name of the perfect or major interval under each example.

- Use "P" for perfect intervals and "Maj" for major intervals.

- Hint for examples on this page: Try counting the number of half steps between the notes, or think of the lower note as the first note of a major scale.

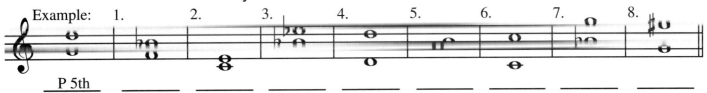

Example: P 5th 1. ___ 2. ___ 3. ___ 4. ___ 5. ___ 6. ___ 7. ___ 8. ___

B
Add the note above the given note that makes the perfect or major interval named in each example.

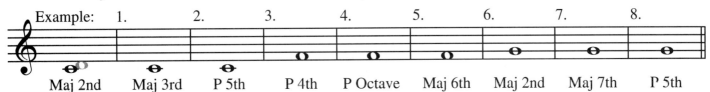

Example: Maj 2nd 1. Maj 3rd 2. P 5th 3. P 4th 4. P Octave 5. Maj 6th 6. Maj 2nd 7. Maj 7th 8. P 5th

C
- Choose either the keyboard or fretboard examples below.

- Write the name of the interval below each keyboard diagram.

- Write the name of the interval below each fretboard diagram.

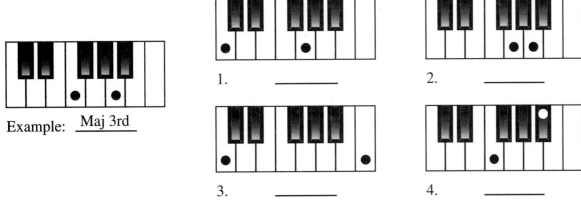

Example: Maj 3rd

1. ___   2. ___

3. ___   4. ___

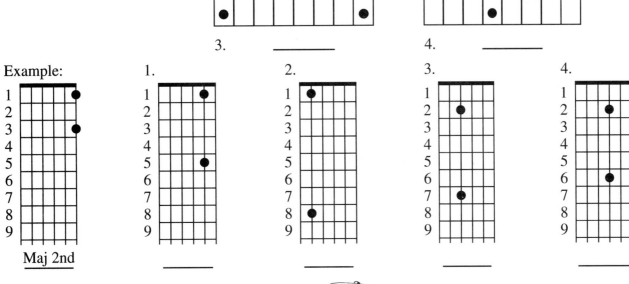

Example: Maj 2nd   1. ___   2. ___   3. ___   4. ___

EAR TRAINING

A

TRACK 6

- Listen to each example.
- If the interval is a perfect 4th, circle "P 4th."
- If the interval is smaller than a perfect 4th, circle "Smaller."
- If the interval is larger than a perfect 4th, circle "Larger."

Example: (P 4th) Smaller   Larger

1.   P 4th   Smaller   Larger

2.   P 4th   Smaller   Larger

3.   P 4th   Smaller   Larger

4.   P 4th   Smaller   Larger

5.   P 4th   Smaller   Larger

B

TRACK 7

- Listen to each example.
- If the interval is a major 6th, circle "Maj 6th."
- If the interval is smaller than a major 6th, circle "Smaller."
- If the interval is larger than a major 6th, circle "Larger."

Example: (Maj 6th)   Smaller   Larger

1.   Maj 6th Smaller   Larger

2.   Maj 6th Smaller   Larger

3.   Maj 6th Smaller   Larger

4.   Maj 6th Smaller   Larger

5.   Maj 6th Smaller   Larger

Intervals—Minor

If you make a major interval smaller by a half step, it becomes a **minor interval**. You can make a major interval minor by lowering the top note with a flat (or, if the note is sharp, with a natural).

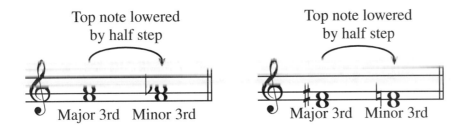

You can also make a major interval smaller by raising the bottom note by a half step. You can do this by raising the bottom note with a sharp (or, if the note is flat, with a natural).

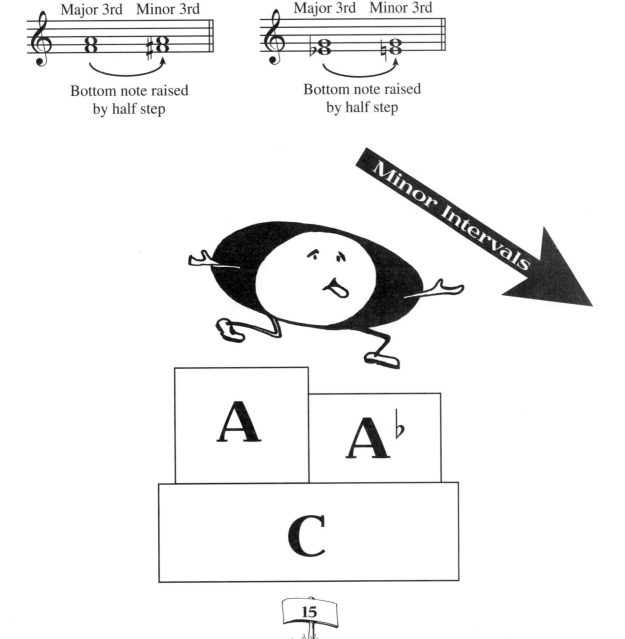

Here are some examples of changing major intervals to minor on the keyboard:

Lowering the top note:

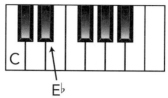

- The distance from C to E is four half steps. This interval is a **major 3rd**.

- The distance from C to E♭ is three half steps. This interval is a **minor 3rd**.

Raising the bottom note:

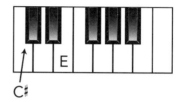

- The distance from C to E is four half steps. This interval is a **major 3rd**.

- The distance from C♯ to E is three half steps. This interval is a **major 3rd**.

Here are some examples of changing major intervals to minor on the guitar. These examples use notes on strings that are next to each other.

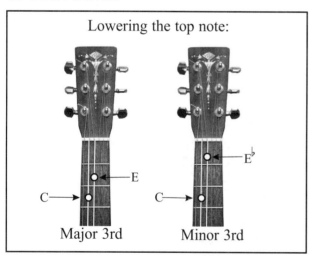

Lowering the top note:

Major 3rd   Minor 3rd

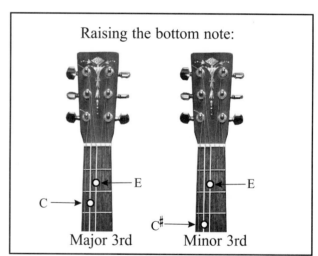

Raising the bottom note:

Major 3rd   Minor 3rd

- The distance from C to E is four half steps. This interval is a **major 3rd**.

- The distance from C to E is four half steps. This interval is a **major 3rd**.

- The distance from C to E♭ is three half steps. This interval is a **minor 3rd**.

- The distance from C♯ to E is three half steps. This interval is a **major 3rd**.

WORKSHEET

A
- Write the name of the interval under each example.
- Use "min" for minor intervals.

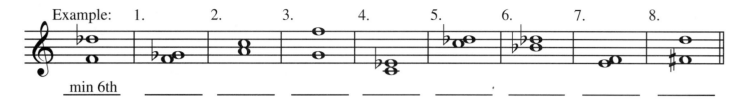

min 6th

B
- Add the note above the given note that makes the interval named in each example.

min 7th   min 3rd   min 6th   min 2nd   min 3rd   min 6th   min 7th   min 2nd   min 3rd

C
- Choose either the keyboard or fretbord diagrams below.
- Write the name of the interval below each keyboard diagram. If the interval is major, make it minor by drawing a new dot. If it is minor, make it major.

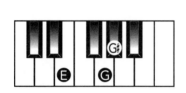

Example: min 3rd
          Maj 3rd

1. _____

2. _____

3. _____

4. _____

- Write the name of the interval below each fretboard diagram. Hint: Find the names of the two notes, stack the higher note on top of the lower note, and count the number of half steps. If the interval is major, make it minor by drawing a new dot. If it is minor, make it major.

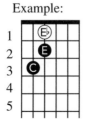

Example:

Maj 3rd

min 3rd

1. _____   2. _____   3. _____   4. _____

EAR TRAINING

TRACK

- Listen to each example.
- If the interval is a major 2nd, circle "Maj 2nd."
- If the interval is a minor 2nd, circle "min 2nd."

Example: Maj 2nd

1. Maj 2nd   min 2nd

2. Maj 2nd   min 2nd

3. Maj 2nd   min 2nd

4. Maj 2nd   min 2nd

5. Maj 2nd   min 2nd

TRACK 9

- Listen to each example.
- If the interval is a major 3rd, circle "Maj 3rd."
- If the interval is a minor 3rd, circle "min 3rd."

Example: Maj 3rd

1. Maj 3rd   min 3rd

2. Maj 3rd   min 3rd

3. Maj 3rd   min 3rd

4. Maj 3rd   min 3rd

5. Maj 3rd   min 3rd

Chords— Major Triads

A **chord** is a group of notes played together. A chord made up of exactly three notes is called a **triad**. There are a few different types of triads; we'll begin by looking at the **major triad**. A major triad is made of the first, third and fifth notes of a major scale. When used in a triad, these notes are called the **root**, **3rd**, and **5th**. If you can write any major scale, you can write any major triad!

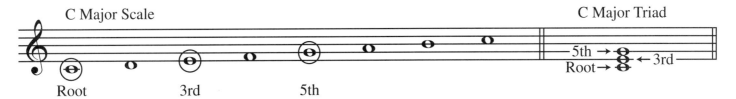

You can also make a major triad using the intervals you learned on page 12. Here's how:

1. Choose any note to be the root.
2. Add the note a major 3rd (four half steps) up from the root.
3. Add the note a perfect 5th (seven half steps) up from the root.

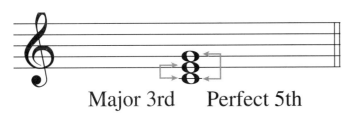

Major 3rd   Perfect 5th

You can also make a major triad by stacking a minor 3rd on top of a major 3rd. These two intervals share the middle note (the 3rd) of the triad.

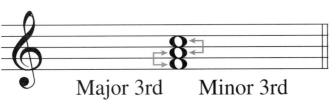

Major 3rd   Minor 3rd

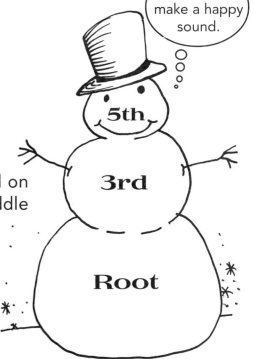

Major triads make a happy sound.

5th

3rd

Root

WORKSHEET

A   Using the given note as the root, write a major triad for each example.

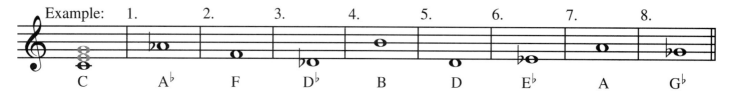

Choose either B or C below.

B   Write the name of the major triad below each keyboard diagram.

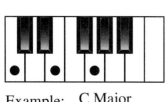

Example: C Major

1. _____

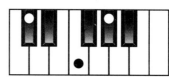

2. _____

3. _____

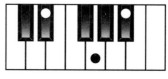

4. _____

C
- Draw the note that's missing from each major triad on the fretboard diagram.

- Write in the name of the missing note.

- Write "R" if the missing note is the root, "3" if it is the 3rd or "5" if it's the 5th.

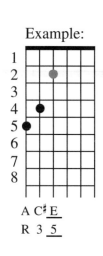

A C♯ E
R 3 5

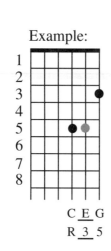

C E G
R 3 5

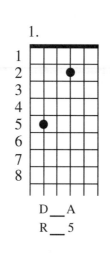

D __ A
R __ 5

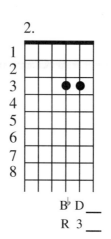

B♭ D __
R 3 __

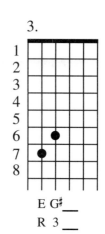

E G♯ __
R 3 __

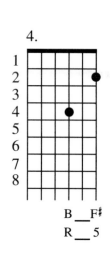

B __ F♯
R __ 5

EAR TRAINING

- Listen to each major chord.
- Sing along on "La."

1. C Major   2. G Major

3. F Major   4. D Major

5. A Major   6. B♭ Major

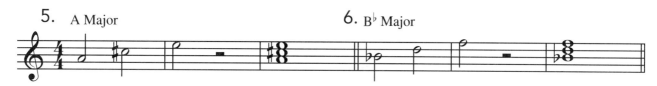

- Listen to each example.
- If the example is a major chord, circle "Major."
- If the example is not a major chord, circle "Other."

Example: (Major) Other

1. Major Other

2. Major Other

3. Major Other

4. Major Other

5. Major Other

Chords— Minor Triads

Like major triads, **minor triads** contain a root, 3rd and 5th. You can make a minor triad by beginning with a major triad and lowering the 3rd by one half step, using a flat (or, if the note is sharp, a natural).

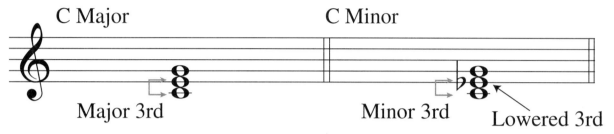

C Major   C Minor

Major 3rd   Minor 3rd   Lowered 3rd

You can also make a minor triad using intervals you've already learned. Here's how:

1. Choose any note to be the root.
2. Add the note a minor 3rd (three half steps) up from the root.
3. Add the note a perfect 5th (seven half steps) up from the root.

Minor 3rd   Perfect 5th

You can also make a minor triad by stacking a major 3rd on top of a minor 3rd. These two intervals share the middle note (the 3rd) of the triad.

Minor 3rd   Major 3rd

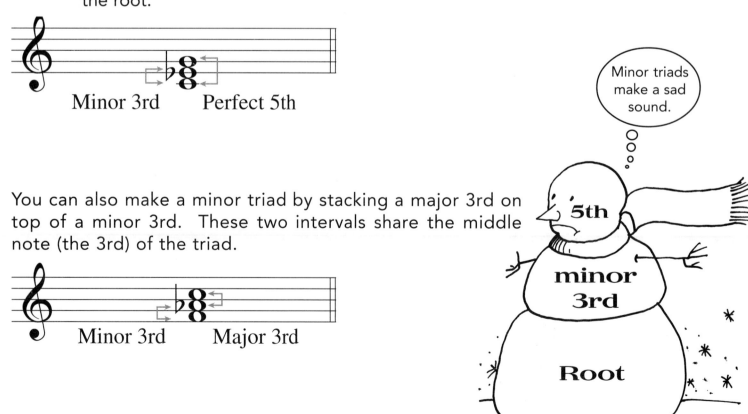

Minor triads make a sad sound.

5th

minor 3rd

Root

WORKSHEET

A   Using the given note as the root, write a minor triad for each example.

Example: 1.   2.   3.   4.   5.   6.   7.   8.

C Minor   F Minor   B♭ Minor   D Minor   F♯ Minor   E Minor   G Minor   A Minor   E♭ Minor

Choose either B or C.

B   Write the name of the minor triad below each keyboard diagram.

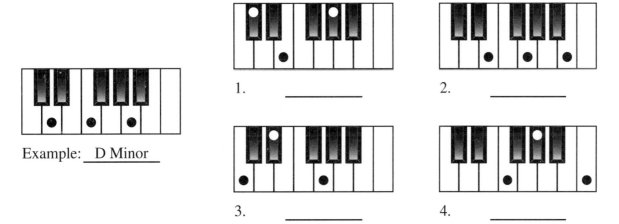

Example: D Minor

1. _____   2. _____

3. _____   4. _____

C   • Draw the note that's missing from each minor triad on the fretboard diagram.

   • Write in the name of the missing note.

   • Write "R" if the missing note is the root, "3" if it is the minor 3rd or "5th" if it's the 5th.

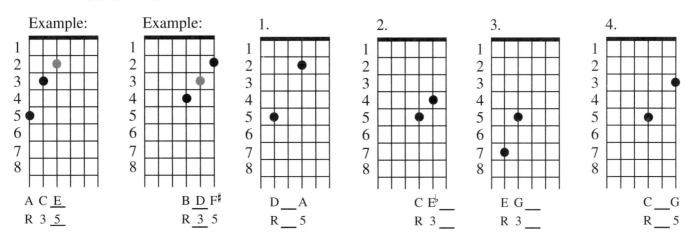

Example: Example: 1.   2.   3.   4.

A C E   B D F♯   D __ A   C E♭ __   E G __   C __ G
R 3 5   R 3 5   R __ 5   R 3 __   R 3 __   R __ 5

EAR TRAINING

- Listen to each minor chord.
- Sing along on "La."

1. C Minor
2. G Minor

3. F Minor
4. D Minor

5. A Minor
6. B♭ Minor

- Listen to each example.
- If the example is a major chord, circle "Major."
- If the example is a minor chord, circle "Minor."

Example: Major   (Minor)

1.   Major   Minor

2.   Major   Minor

3.   Major   Minor

4.   Major   Minor

5.   Major   Minor

REVIEW

A   Unlock this exercise by drawing a line from each key to its key signature.

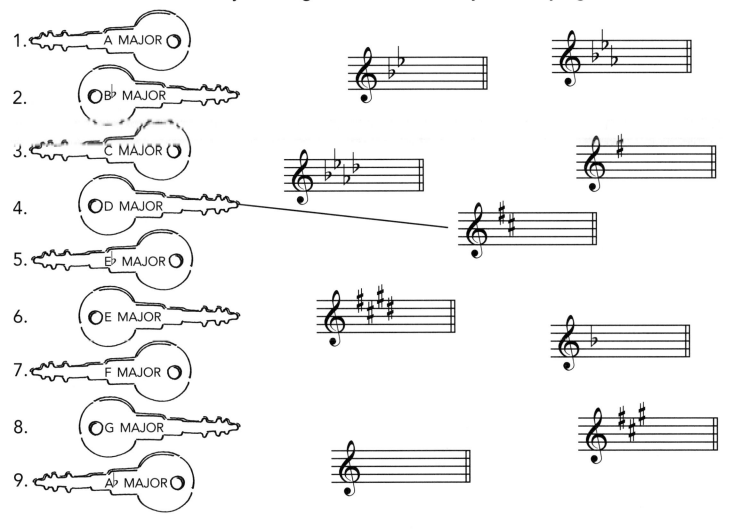

1. A MAJOR
2. B♭ MAJOR
3. C MAJOR
4. D MAJOR
5. E♭ MAJOR
6. E MAJOR
7. F MAJOR
8. G MAJOR
9. A♭ MAJOR

B   • Write the correct key signature on the staff for each example.

   • Watch out for the clef change!

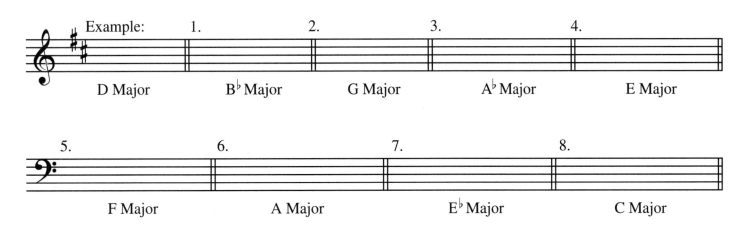

Example: D Major   1. B♭ Major   2. G Major   3. A♭ Major   4. E Major

5. F Major   6. A Major   7. E♭ Major   8. C Major

25

REVIEW

A • Identify the major or minor triad in each example.

    • Hint: If the bottom two notes make a major 3rd, it's a major triad; if the bottom two notes make a minor 3rd, it's a minor triad.

    • Watch out for the clef change.

F Minor

B • Draw a major or minor triad on the staff for each example.

    • Use the given note as the root.

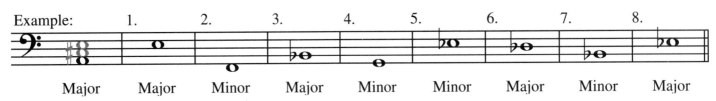

Major   Major   Minor   Major   Minor   Minor   Major   Minor   Major

C • Identify the interval in each example.

    • Use "P" for perfect, "Maj" for major and "min" for minor.

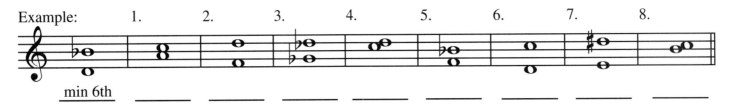

min 6th

D • Add the note above the given note that makes the interval named in each example.

    • Hint: Count half steps to find the correct note.

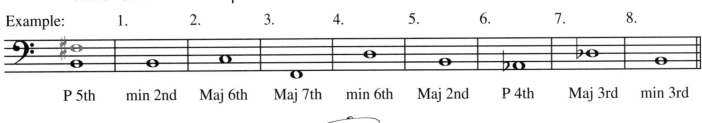

P 5th   min 2nd   Maj 6th   Maj 7th   min 6th   Maj 2nd   P 4th   Maj 3rd   min 3rd

SIXTEENTH NOTES

You already know four kinds of note and rest values:

Whole Note and Rest   o ▬   = Four beats in $\frac{4}{4}$

Half Note and Rest   ♩ ▬   = Two beats in $\frac{4}{4}$

Quarter Note and Rest   ♩ 𝄽   = One beat in $\frac{4}{4}$

Eighth Note and Rest   ♪ ﹆   = One half beat in $\frac{4}{4}$

You've probably noticed that we divide each note value by two to get the next smaller kind of note. For example, a whole note (four beats) divided by two equals a half note (two beats).

An eighth note is the smallest note value you've learned so far, but there are even smaller values. When you divide an eighth note in two, you get a **sixteenth note**. Since there are two sixteenths in an eighth note, there are four sixteenths in a quarter note. Note that sixteenth notes have two flags.

When more than one sixteenth note is used in a row, or sixteenth notes are used with eighth notes, they are usually joined with beams. Since sixteenth notes have two flags, they also use two beams.

A good way to count sixteenth notes is like this: 1 e & a, 2 e & a ("One-ee-and-ah, two-ee-and-ah"), etc. Try saying this rhythm out loud as in the example below. Notice how the notes are beamed.

1 e & a 2 e & a 3 e & a 4 e & a

Dotted Notes

You already know about extending a note's length by tying it to another note, but there's *another* way to make a note longer: Put a dot next to it! Adding a dot increases a note's value by half. It's a lot like a simple math problem. For example, let's begin with a half note:

- How long is a half note? Two beats.
- How much value does a dot add to a note? Half of the note's value.
- What's half of a half note? A quarter note, or one beat.
- What's a half note (two beats) plus a quarter note (one beat)? Three beats.

So, a dotted half note equals three beats!

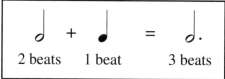

Here's an example of dotted half notes in $\frac{4}{4}$ time:

Dots work the same way with dotted quarter notes.

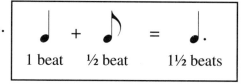

Dotted quarters are usually followed by eighth notes. Here are some dotted quarter notes in $\frac{4}{4}$ time:

It works the same with dotted eighth notes.

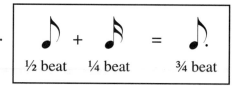

Dotted eighth notes are usually followed by sixteenth notes. Here are some dotted eighth notes in $\frac{3}{4}$ time. Notice that dotted eighths and sixteenths are beamed together:

WORKSHEET

A 1. In ¾, one dotted half note equals _____ beats.

2. In ¾, eight sixteenth notes equal _____ beats.

3. One dotted quarter note equals _____ eighth notes.

4. One dotted eighth note equals _____ sixteenth notes.

B • Add sixteenth notes to the gray boxes to fill each measure with the correct number of beats.

• Write the beat count under each measure.

• For dotted eighth notes and sixteenth notes, use "1 e & a," etc.

• If you like, use "+" instead of "&."

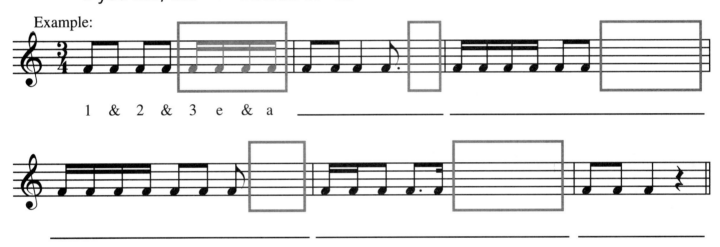

C • Draw in the missing barlines to give each measure the correct number of beats.

• Don't forget to look at the time signature!

EAR TRAINING

TRACK 14

- Listen to each example.
- Circle the letter of the rhythmic passage that matches each example you hear.

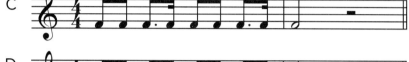

Example: A   B   C   ⓓ   E

1. A   B   C   D   E   3. A   B   C   D   E

2. A   B   C   D   E   4. A   B   C   D   E

TRACK 15

- Part of the melody is missing!
- Each example completes the melody in a different way.
- Circle the letter of the note or notes that complete the melody in each example.

Example: Ⓐ   B   C   D   E

1. A   B   C   D   E

2. A   B   C   D   E

3. A   B   C   D   E

4. A   B   C   D   E

⅜ Time

As you know, the number on the bottom of a time signature tells you what note value gets one beat, while the top number tells you how many beats are in a measure. In $\frac{4}{4}$, for example, a quarter note gets one beat, and there are four beats per measure. In $\frac{6}{8}$, things work a little differently.

You can look at this time signature in the old, tried and true way:

However, most music written in $\frac{6}{8}$ doesn't *feel* this way. The feeling of beat patterns in music is called **meter.** In $\frac{4}{4}$, $\frac{3}{4}$ and $\frac{2}{4}$, each beat can be divided by into halves (eighth notes), as when you count "1 & 2 & 3 & 4 &." This kind of meter, with a pattern of two eighth notes per beat, is called **simple meter.**

In $\frac{6}{8}$ time, the eighth notes are usually in a pattern of *three* per beat. This pattern is called **compound meter.** The six eighth notes in a measure of $\frac{6}{8}$ are in two groups of three, counted "1 & a 2 & a." In fact, the feel of most music in $\frac{6}{8}$ is two beats per measure, not six.

The dotted quarter note you learned about on page 28 comes in handy for $\frac{6}{8}$ time. Since a dotted quarter note is equal to three eighth notes, you can see how it is the perfect note value for $\frac{6}{8}$ time.

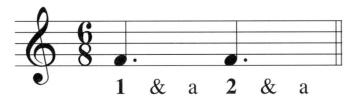

WORKSHEET

A • Add the beat count under each measure, using "1 & a, 2 & a."

• Make sure each beat lines up with the correct notes.

• If you like, use "+" instead of "&."

1 & a   2 & a   _____   _____

_____   _____   _____

B • Draw in the missing barlines to give each measure the correct number of beats.

• Don't forget to look at the time signature!

EAR TRAINING

TRACK 16

- Listen to each example.

- Circle the letter of the melody that matches each example you hear.

A

B

C

D

E

Example: A   B   Ⓒ   D   E

1. A   B   C   D   E   3. A   B   C   D   E

2. A   B   C   D   E   4. A   B   C   D   E

TRACK 17

- Listen to each example.

- If the melody sounds like it could be in 6/8 (two groups of three beats per measure), circle "6/8."

- If the melody doesn't sound like it could be in 6/8, circle "Other."

Example: ⑥/⑧   Other

1.   6/8   Other

2.   6/8   Other

3.   6/8   Other

4.   6/8   Other

Dynamic and Tempo Markings

The music you play usually contains hints that will help you create a musical mood. These hints are often given as **dynamic** and **tempo** markings. Dynamic markings are the volume controls of music. They tell you how loud or soft the music should be. Tempo markings are the speed controls of music. They tell you how fast or slow the music should be.

A long time ago, Italian became the language of music all over the world. Most dynamic and tempo markings come from Italian words. Look at the charts below and see if you can find any of these markings in music you know.

Dynamic Markings

ppp	*pianississimo*	Very, very soft
pp	*pianissimo*	Very soft
p	*piano*	Soft
mp	*mezzo piano*	Medium soft
mf	*mezzo forte*	Medium loud
f	*forte*	Loud
ff	*fortissmo*	Very loud
fff	*fortississimo*	Very, very loud
<	*crescendo*	Gradually getting louder (abbr. *cresc.*)
>	*decrescendo*	Gradually getting softer (abbr. *decresc.*)

Tempo Markings

Largo	Very, very slow
Lento	Very slow
Adagio	Slow
Andante	"Walking" tempo
Moderato	Moderate
Allegretto	On the quick side
Allegro	Fast
Presto	Very fast
Prestissimo	As fast as possible
Ritardanto (rit.)	Slowing down
Accelerando	Speeding up

Articulation Markings

Articulation markings are symbols that tell you how a single note or group of notes should be played. Like dynamic and tempo markings, they add meaning to the music and help to create the mood.

Try playing your favorite piece, but play all the notes very short. How does the music sound? Happy? Exciting? Scary? Try to think of your own words to describe this sound. Now, play the same song with all the notes smoothly connected. How does it sound now? You can see (and hear) that different articulations can make a very big difference in sound.

Here are some of the most important articulation markings. See if you can find any of them in music you know.

Articulation Markings

∧	Marcato	Acented, stressed
>	Accent	Play the note a little louder
.	Staccato	Play the note short
–	Tenuto	Hold the note for its full value
-	Mezzo Staccato	Play the note short, but not quite as short as staccato. Slightly detached.
⌢	Fermata	Hold the note longer than its normal value
⊓	Down bow	Bow, pluck or strum down (toward the floor)
V	Up bow	Bow, pluck or strum up (toward the ceiling)

Here's how some of these markings look in a musical score:

Repeats

This is a **repeat sign.** :|

When you come to a repeat sign in a piece of music, it means that you should go back to the beginning of the piece and play from there.

Sometimes, only part of a piece is repeated. When that happens, two repeat signs surround the part that you play again. The first one has dots that face right, and the second one has dots that face left. When you reach the second repeat sign, go back to the first one and play from there. When you reach the second repeat sign again, continue playing as usual, unless it is the end of the piece.

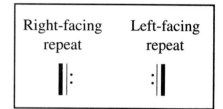

Repeat this measure.   Then play this.

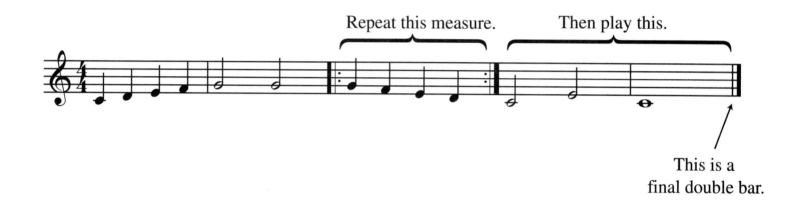

This is a
final double bar.

Sometimes, a section of a piece will be repeated, but the end will be different the second time. The music that you play at the end of the section the first time is called a **first ending**, which is marked with a bracket and "1."

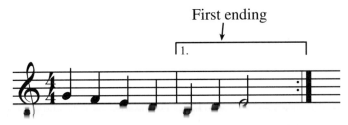

First ending

After playing the first ending, go back to the beginning (or the right-facing repeat sign, if there is one) and play from there. When you reach the first ending, skip it and play the second ending instead.

Skip this the second time.　　　Play this the second time.

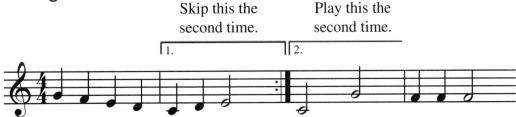

When a second ending comes at the end of a piece, it works the same way, only it looks slightly different.

Bracket comes down

Final double bar

Da Capo, Coda ⊕, Fine, Dal Segno

Using repeat signs is just one way that musicians save paper. On this page, you'll learn a few more.

Sometimes, you'll see the phrase *Da Capo al Fine.* (Say: "Da COP-oh Al FEE-nay.") This phrase, which is abbreviated "D.C. al Fine," is Italian for "go back to the beginning (*Capo*) and play to the end (*Fine*)." You'll usually find *Fine*, which is where you'll stop, near a **double bar** (two thin lines).

Fine ← End here the second time

Go back to the beginning → D.C. al Fine

Da Capo al Coda ("Da COP-oh Al KOH-da"), abbreviated "D.C. al Coda," is Italian for "go back to the beginning and play to the **coda** (ending section)." When you see this phrase, go back to the beginning and play until you see the coda sign. Then, skip to near the end of the piece, where you'll find another coda sign, and play from there.

Skip to the coda the second time ↘ To Coda ⊕

Go back to the beginning → D. C. al Coda

⊕ Coda

Dal Segno al Fine, which is abbreviated "D.S. al Fine," is Italian for "Go to the sign and play to the end." This is a way to repeat a section of the piece that is not at the beginning. When you see this phrase, look earlier in the piece for this sign 𝄋, and play from there to the *Fine.*

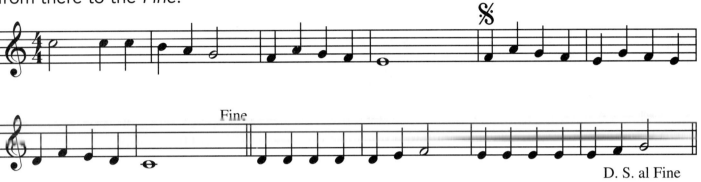

Dal Segno al Coda, which is abbreviated "D.S. al Coda," is similar to D.S. al Fine. When you see this phrase, look earlier in the piece for this sign 𝄋, and play from there to the coda sign. Then, skip to near the end of the piece where you'll find another coda sign, and play from there.

WORKSHEET

A • Follow the steps to practice drawing the sign 𝄋.

• Try drawing the sign in the boxes below.

B • Write out "Ode to Joy" in a way that uses fewer measures.

• Use "D. S. al Fine," "Fine" and the sign 𝄋.

• Hint: Look for a part that happens twice in the same way.

ODE TO JOY

Ludwig van Beethoven

Write your version here.

EAR TRAINING

TRACK 18

- Listen to each example.
- Place staccato dots under the notes that are played short.

Example

TRACK 19

- Listen to each example.
- Write the missing dynamic markings in the boxes under each example.
- Use only *p*, *f*, < and > .

Example

Review

A   Use lines to join all the values with the same number of beats.

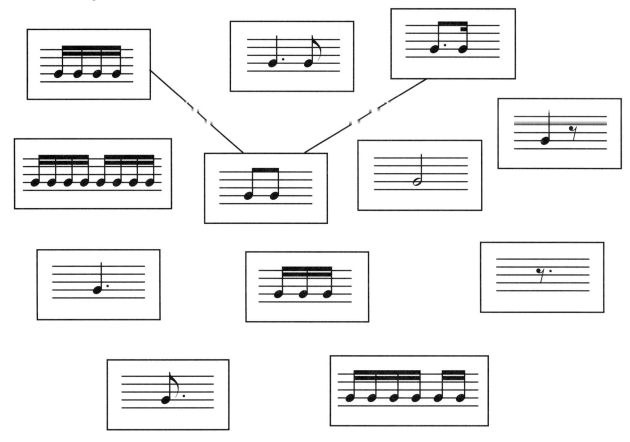

B
- Try writing your own rhythm composition in ⁶⁄₈.
- Make your composition eight measures long.
- Use the same pitch throughout.
- Use a combination of eighth notes and rests, quarter notes and rests, and dotted quarter notes.
- Be sure that each measure contains the correct number of beats.

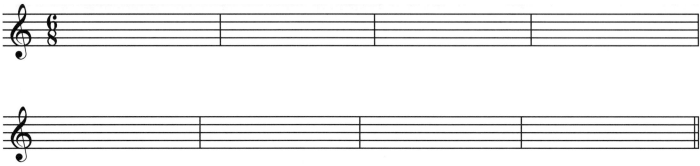

Review

A Place these tempo markings in order from slowest to fastest.

Presto	Adagio	Allegro
Andante	Allegretto	Lento

1. _____   2. _____   3. _____

4. _____   5. _____   6. _____

B Match each dynamic marking with the sound it best describes.

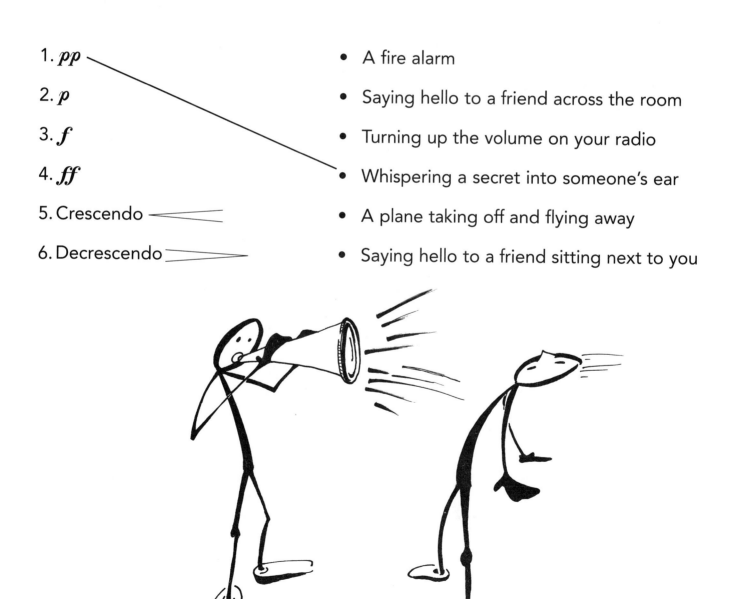

1. *pp*

2. *p*

3. *f*

4. *ff*

5. Crescendo

6. Decrescendo

- A fire alarm

- Saying hello to a friend across the room

- Turning up the volume on your radio

- Whispering a secret into someone's ear

- A plane taking off and flying away

- Saying hello to a friend sitting next to you

ANSWER KEY

Page 5:

1. C Major
2. G Major — 5th
3. D Major — 5th
4. A Major — 5th
5. E Major — 5th

Page 6: B 1. 5th 2. Smaller 3. Larger 4. 5th 5. 5th

Page 9:

1. B♭ Major   2. D Major   3. A♭ Major
4. E♭ Major   5. B Major   6. E Major

Page 10: A

1. Key: D Major   2. Key: A Major
3. Key: E Major

B A.   B.   C.
D.   E.

1. B 2. E 3. D 4. A

Page 13: A

P 5th P 4th Maj 3rd P 4th P Octave Maj 2nd P Octave Maj 6th Maj 7th

B

Maj 2nd Maj 3rd P 5th P 4th P Octave Maj 6th Maj 2nd Maj 7th P 5th

C 1. P 5th 2. Maj 2nd 3. P Octave 4. P 4th

1. Maj 3rd 2. P 5th 3. P 4th 4. Maj 3rd

Page 14: A 1. P 4th 2. Larger 3. P 4th 4. Smaller 5. P 4th

B 1. Smaller 2. Maj 6th 3. Maj 6th 4. Smaller 5. Larger

ANSWER KEY

Page 17: A

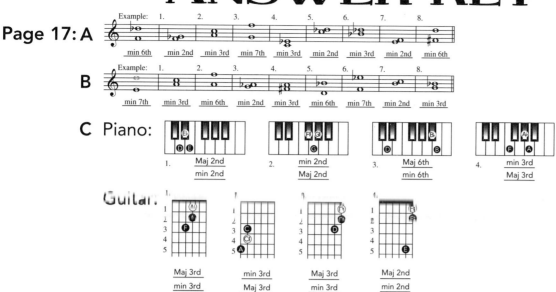

min 6th · min 2nd · min 3rd · min 7th · min 3rd · min 2nd · min 3rd · min 2nd · min 6th

B

min 7th · min 3rd · min 6th · min 2nd · min 3rd · min 6th · min 7th · min 2nd · min 3rd

C Piano:

1. Maj 2nd / min 2nd
2. min 2nd / Maj 2nd
3. Maj 6th / min 6th
4. min 3rd / Maj 3rd

Guitar:

1. Maj 3rd / min 3rd
2. min 3rd / Maj 3rd
3. Maj 3rd / min 3rd
4. Maj 2nd / min 2nd

Page 18: A 1. Maj 2nd 2. min 2nd 3. Maj 2nd 4. Maj 2nd 5. min 2nd

B 1. min 3rd 2. Maj 3rd 3. min 3rd 4. Maj 3rd 5. Maj 3rd

Page 20: A

C · A♭ · F · D♭ · B · D · E♭ · A · G♭

B 1. E Major 2. D♭ Major (or C♯ Major) 3. F Major 4. E♭ Major

C

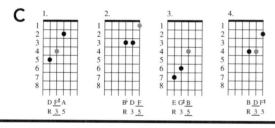

1. D F♯ A R 3 5
2. B♭ D F R 3 5
3. E G♯ B R 3 5
4. B D F♯ R 3 5

Page 21: B 1. Other 2. Major 3. Major 4. Other 5. Major

Page 23: A

Cmin · Fmin · B♭min · Dmin · F♯min · Emin · Gmin · Amin · E♭min

B 1. C♯ Minor (or D♭ Minor) 2. E Minor 3. C Minor 4. F Minor

C

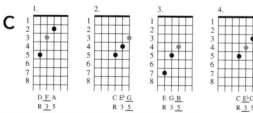

1. D F A R 3 5
2. C E♭ G R 3 5
3. E G B R 3 5
4. C E♭ G R 3 5

Page 24: B 1. Major 2. Minor 3. Minor 4. Major 5. Minor

Page 25: A 1. A MAJOR 2. B♭ MAJOR 3. C MAJOR 4. D MAJOR 5. E♭ MAJOR 6. E MAJOR 7. F MAJOR 8. G MAJOR 9. A♭ MAJOR

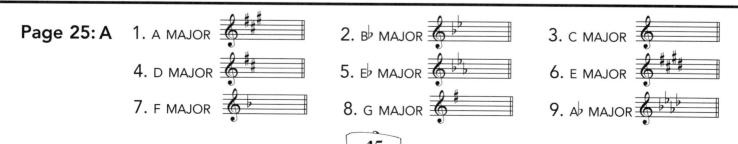

ANSWER KEY

Page 25: B

D Major   B♭ Major   G Major   A♭ Major   E Major

F Major   A Major   E♭ Major   C Major

Page 26: A 1. G Major 2. E♭ Minor 3. B Minor 4. D Major

5. C Minor 6. A Minor 7. E Major 8. D♭ Major

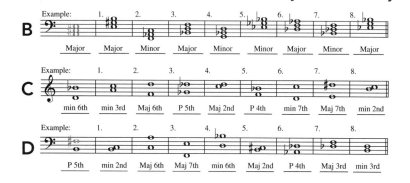

B Major Major Minor Major Minor Minor Major Minor Major

C min 6th min 3rd Maj 6th P 5th Maj 2nd P 4th min 7th Maj 7th min 2nd

D P 5th min 2nd Maj 6th Maj 7th min 6th Maj 2nd P 4th Maj 3rd min 3rd

---

Page 29: A 1. <u>3</u> 2. <u>2</u> 3. <u>3</u> 4. <u>3</u>

B

1 & 2 & 3 e & a   1 & 2 3e& a   1 e & a 2 & 3 e & a

1 e & a 2 & 3e & a   1 e &a 2e& a 3 e & a   1 & 2 3

C

Page 30: A 1. A 2. B 3. C 4. E   **B** 1. E 2. D 3. B 4. C

Page 32: A

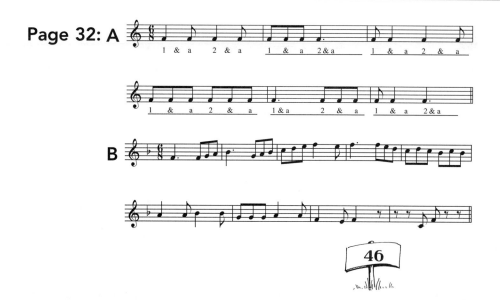

1 & a 2 & a   1 & a 2 & a   1 & a 2 & a

1 & a 2 & a   1 & a 2 & a   1 & a 2 & a

B

ANSWER KEY

Page 33: **A** 1. D 2. E 3. B 4. A

B 1. Other 2. § 3. § 4. Other

Page 40: B

D. S. al Fine

Page 41: A

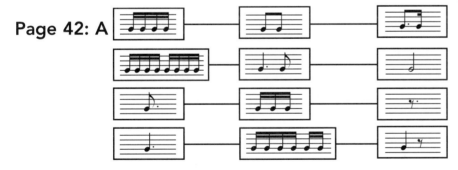

Page 42: A

B Answers will vary.

Page 43: A 1. Lento 2. Adagio 3. Andante 4. Allegretto 5. Allegro 6. Presto

B 1. Whispering a secret into someone's ear
2. Saying hello to a friend sitting next to you
3. Saying hello to a friend across the room
4. A fire alarm
5. Turning up the volume on your radio
6. A plane taking off and flying away